C000318924

fondue

Written by Christine Smith

KUDOS

Published by Kudos, an imprint of Top That! Publishing plc.
Copyright © 2004 Top That! Publishing plc,
Tide Mill Way, Woodbridge, Suffolk, IP12 IAP, www.kudosbooks.com

Kudos is a Trademark of Top That! Publishing plc

All rights reserved

CONTENTS

WHAT IS FONDUE?

The word 'fondue' derives from the French **'fondre'**, meaning to melt or to blend. The story goes that the idea of a fondue originated in the 18th century, high in the Swiss Alps, where villagers had only cheese, bread and wine readily available as sustenance during the long winter months. As winter dragged on, the summer-made cheese became harder, but when melted with wine and a little cherry brandy, or kirsch, became a wonderfully tasty and filling meal with chunks of bread dipped in to scoop up the warm mixture. In peasant villages, people may only have made bread once a week, and so after a few days the bread would have been stale, but ideal for dunking in the fondue.

A communal pot called a 'caquelon' was used. This heavy earthenware pot protected the cheese from burning and kept the fondue warm for eating, long forks being used to dunk the bread into the melted cheese. So a whole cuisine was born out of necessity, and one which today has been developed in all sorts of exciting directions.

Cheese Fondues ◀
Fish Fondues ◀
Vegetable Fondues ◀
Meat Fondues ◀
Sweet Fondues ◀
Simple Sauces ◀
Savoury Dips ◀
Sweet Dippers ◀

SWITZERLAND'S NATIONAL DISH

The fondue has now become the national dish of Switzerland, and traditionally Emmental and Gruyère cheese are used together. The combination of cheeses produces a flavour that is neither too bland nor sharp, and a texture that is neither lumpy nor stringy. A dry white wine is added, which helps to keep the direct heat away from the cheeses and helps to blend them together smoothly, as well as adding flavour. Cherry brandy, or kirsch is also used, especially if the cheese is young and bland.

Different regions of Switzerland have their own variations on the classic recipe.

In Geneva, for example, it is common to use three cheeses, Gruyère, Emmental and Walliser Berghase, while in Vaud, chopped, roasted garlic is added to Gruyère cheese.

In Glarus, a roux made from butter, flour, and milk is first made, to which the cheese is added. This helps to prevent the cheese from separating as it is heated.

EUROPEAN VARIATIONS

The French have the Fondue Bourguignonne (p. 74), where strips of fillet steak are dipped in hot oil to cook quickly, and are then dipped in a savoury sauce.

Another lovely variation, this time from the Piedmont region of Italy, is Bagna Cauda (p. 56). This is made from warming together butter, olive oil, anchovies and garlic. Again, chunks of crisp bread or vegetables are then used to scoop up this wonderful savoury mixture.

IDEAS FOR FONDUE HAVE GROWN SINCE THE DAYS OF ITS SWISS ORIGINS

A TASTE OF THE ORIENT

From the Orient, there is the Mongolian Hotpot or Fondue Chinoise, where seafood or meat is cooked in hot stock. This originates from the Szechuan cuisine of China (p. 58).

Pieces of food are picked up with chopsticks and plunged into a pot of boiling stock. Depending on the size, the pieces are either left to cook before being picked out again, or for small pieces of food, they are simply held in the stock until ready. Often there are two pots of stock: one spicily hot, the other mild.

The Japanese tempura involves pieces of vegetables, meat or fish being dipped in a light batter and then put into hot oil to fry.

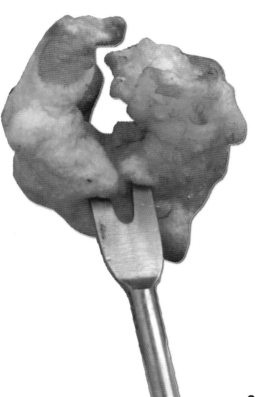

FONDUE FACTS AND TIPS

Fondue is a wonderful communal eating experience, and fondue parties are definitely enjoying a comeback. Having been very popular in the '60s and '70s, sales of fondue pots and equipment are now booming again as people find out for themselves what a fun, easy, yet impressive, and even luxurious way it is to entertain friends and family. A fondue pot can prove a great ice-breaker among people who do not know each other very well.

HOW TO EAT A FONDUE

Here are a few basic guidelines for eating fondue. To eat a cheese fondue, spear a piece of bread and dip it into the fondue, swirling it around in a figure of eight. Let it drip for a moment or two over the pot before eating, to allow the excess fondue to fall back into the pot, and also to allow the cheese to cool slightly.

With a meat or fish fondue, spear the piece of meat or fish and plunge into the hot oil or stock until it is cooked. Remove, allow it to drip over the pot, and then slide it off the fondue fork with a dining fork. Use the second fork to dip the cooked meat or fish into the sauce you have, and eat.

DRINKS WITH FONDUE

There are some traditions associated with what to drink with a fondue. It is often thought that drinking cold drinks with hot food, particularly warm, melted cheese, causes indigestion, so warm fruit juice, mulled wine, and warm tea are usual accompaniments to a cheese fondue, with a small glass of kirsch served between courses.

Alternatively, you may like to serve a dry white wine, perhaps at room temperature, but never serve ice-cold drinks. With meat or fish fondues, serve the appropriate red, rosé, or white wine, or perhaps lager or cider. Sweet fondues go very well with a sweet liqueur or a sweet, sparkling wine.

FONDUE WITH CHEESE

Lots of different cheeses can be used, but it is important to choose the correct combination: one that is good for melting, gives a smooth consistency, and a good balance of flavours – Emmental, Gruyère, Edam, Gouda, cheddar, Parmesan, Pecorino and Fontina are all commonly used. But you can use Camembert, Pont l'Eveque, Comte, Beaufort, Manchego, soft goats' cheese, among others, and the recipes in the cheese section give an idea of the possibilities.

Having chosen the cheeses for your fondue, you will need to think about the dippers. The traditional dipper is a chunk of crusty French bread on a long fork. This absorbs the flavour, and is nice and chewy in contrast to the smooth fondue.

Make sure that each chunk of bread has a bit of crust as this helps it to stay on

the fork. Also, if the bread is one day old, the firmer texture means the bread is less likely to fall off the fork – and hence risk a forfeit for its owner!

But why stop there? Rye bread is dark and savoury and goes well with a rich, classic Swiss fondue. Naan breads and pitta breads can also be used – they split easily, and can also be cut into strips, ideal for direct dipping without a fork. Italian breadsticks are another way of avoiding the need for long forks and can be dunked directly into the fondue and swirled around. You can also toast the bread, or make it into crostinis by brushing with olive oil and baking on a tray in a medium oven for 5–10 minutes until golden brown.

A cheese fondue can be eaten with lots of other types of dippers – vegetables like carrot sticks, firm tomato chunks, pepper strips, raw courgette, tiny cooked new potatoes, or thick, chunky fries.

slices of crisp apple or pear are good with cheese fondues – try spearing a thin slice of apple and a chunk of French bread on the same fork before dipping. Prawns, pieces of sausage or salami are also possibilities.

For the best results, prepare the fondue in a saucepan on the cooker before transferring it to the fondue pot to keep warm on the table. As the cheese melts in the wine, a dash of lemon juice can help melt the cheese completely. Stir the melting mixture in a figure of eight with a wooden spoon.

If the cheese starts to separate, just keep stirring until it melts together. Do not let it boil, but cook very slowly, and never rush a fondue as it spoils easily. When the fondue is ready, transfer to the fondue pot on top of the table burner, and adjust the heat so that the fondue bubbles away gently.

A cut clove of garlic can be rubbed around the inside of the fondue pot before adding the melted cheese. This will give a hint of garlic, which can really help enhance the flavour of a bland cheese.

Be careful while keeping a cheese fondue warm. If the heat is too high, the cheese will become stringy and lose its creamy texture. You will find with a cheese fondue that, as the fondue keeps warm on the table burner, a crust forms at the bottom of the pot. This is a delicacy to be shared with everyone!

If the fondue becomes too thick during the meal, add a little extra warmed wine or cider. To thicken a fondue that is too thin, make a paste of a little cornflour mixed with water or wine and stir in to thicken over the heat. Add the same if the fondue starts to curdle, along with a squeeze of lemon juice.

MEAT, FISH, AND VEGETABLES

A meat fondue involves strips of raw meat being cooked at the table in hot oil or boiling stock. The oil needs to be at a temperature of about 160°C (350°F). To test for this, carefully put a cube of bread into the oil, and it should brown in thirty seconds. Since the meat is cooked quickly, you will need to use the tender cuts, like fillet steak, lamb, or pork fillet. You can also use strips of chicken breast. The strips of meat can be marinated first – garlic, lemon juice, olive oil, herbs and spices can all be used. A marinade also helps to tenderise the meat before cooking. Once the meat is cooked, it can then be dipped in a relish or sauce.

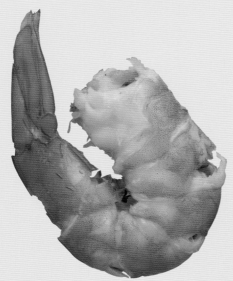

With fish, use a firm variety that will not disintegrate while cooking – monkfish, cod, salmon and haddock will all work well. Large prawns and other seafood such as scallops are good to use as well. Vegetables can also be cooked in a hot oil or stock fondue.

After using a stock to cook fish or vegetables, other ingredients like noodles, bean sprouts, or finely shredded vegetables can be added to the pot to turn the stock into a soup.

SWEET FONDUE

Following the main course fondue with a 'dessert' fondue makes sense, as by this time your guests will be well practised at spearing their food. The simplest is a chocolate fondue, which can be used with all manner of dippers – marshmallows, macaroons or tiny meringues for a really sweet experience; whole strawberries, cherries, mango or pineapple for a fruity effect. There are lots of other ideas featured later for fruit: caramel, custard or cream-based fondues.

It is probably best to have no more than eight people sharing a fondue, but of course you could have a fondue buffet to cater for more people, if you are able to borrow pots from friends.

Be well organised by preparing as much as possible in advance. The dippers can be made and then covered and kept in the fridge. Bread can be cut into chunks or strips and set out in baskets, other sauces and relishes put out beforehand.

FONDUE EQUIPMENT

THE POT

There are lots of different types of fondue pots available. The traditional pot is a heavy earthenware pot called a caquelon. There are, however, several different types of pots available, which are suited to different types of fondue.

A metal pot, either stainless steel or copper with a separate porcelain insert, can be used for cheese fondues and chocolate and other sweet fondues. This type of pot is heavy, transmits heat evenly and retains the heat to keep the fondue warm without burning. If you remove the porcelain insert, you can then use the pot for meat or fish fondues where oil or stock is heated to cook the food, as the metal transmits the heat more quickly to heat up the oil or stock.

Some pots are made of heavy enamelled cast iron and can be used for all types of fondue. They are especially useful for hot oil fondues where it is important to have a heavy, sturdy pot. They are very attractive on the table as well as being quite stable. Electric fondue pots are also available in the shops.

Lastly, simple earthenware pots which have an integral space underneath to hold a candle tea light are ideal for a chocolate fondue, where not much heat is needed.

THE BURNER

Most fondue pots, apart from the electric and simple earthenware type, are sold with a stand which contains a burner. The burner will either run on a solid fuel block which is replaced when needed, or on liquid alcohol fuel.

It is possible to improvise, especially with cheese or sweet fondues, if you have a table warmer which works using tea lights. Use a heavy pan and make the fondue on your cooker first, then you can use the table warmer to keep the fondue warm.

FONDUE FORKS

Fondue pots are usually sold in sets, with the burner and also the long-handled forks for spearing the dippers. The forks usually have two serrated prongs for picking up the food, and heat-resistant handles. It is a good idea to have lots of forks available. Different coloured handles help the guests to know which is theirs.

You can use bamboo skewers as a substitute, and it is traditional with the Mongolian Hotpot to use chopsticks for picking up the food and plunging it into the boiling stock. Smaller pieces of food are held in the stock, while cooking; larger pieces are left to cook and then lifted out with a draining spoon.

CHEESE FONDUE

CONTENTS

CLASSIC SWISS FONDUE

This is the classic combination of cheeses for a Swiss cheese fondue. The lemon juice and cornflour help the cheese to melt evenly and stay smooth. Crusty French bread is the usual accompaniment for dipping, but for a change you could try pieces of brioche, long breadsticks or grissini, which you can dip directly into the melted cheese.

YOU WILL NEED

½ clove garlic

250 ml (8 fl oz) dry white wine

1 tsp lemon juice

225 g (8 oz) grated Gruyère cheese

225 g (8 oz) grated Emmental cheese

1 tsp cornflour

1 tbsp kirsch or cherry brandy

TO SERVE

Cubes of French bread

SERVES 4

1. Rub the inside of the fondue pot with the cut clove of garlic. Put the wine and lemon juice into the fondue pot and heat over a medium heat on your stove top until bubbling.

2. Reduce the heat and carefully stir in the grated cheese. Keep stirring until all the cheese is melted and well combined. This takes a long time, but do not be tempted to turn up the heat, just keep stirring.

3. Blend the cornflour with the kirsch in a small bowl and then add to the cheese mixture. Cook for another two or three minutes, stirring constantly. Do not let the fondue boil.

4. Transfer to the table burner and serve.

* *If your fondue pot does not go on top of your cooker, you can make it in a saucepan instead and then transfer it to the fondue pot before bringing it to the table.*

THIS SIMPLE VARIATION ON THE CLASSIC THEME USES CAERPHILLY CHEESE ALONG WITH VEGETABLES TO CREATE A MORE SUBSTANTIAL FONDUE

WELSH FONDUE

This simple variation on the classic theme uses Caerphilly cheese along with vegetables to create a more substantial fondue. If you cannot get Caerphilly cheese, you could substitute another cheese, such as Cheshire or Lancashire.

1. Put the butter into a saucepan and melt over a low heat. Add the leeks, cover the pan, and cook gently for 10–15 minutes until very soft. Take care not to brown the leeks.

2. Add the flour, mix well, and stir over the heat for a minute to cook through.

3. Add the beer gradually, and cook until thickened, stirring all the time.

4. Add the cheese gradually and continue to cook. Gently stir constantly until the cheese has melted. Season with black pepper.

5. Pour into the fondue pot and serve with the cubes of bread for dipping.

YOU WILL NEED

25 g (1 oz) butter

225 g (8 oz) leeks, trimmed and finely chopped

40 g (1½ oz) plain flour

250 ml (8 fl oz) beer

300 g (10 oz) Caerphilly cheese, grated

freshly ground black pepper

TO SERVE

Cubes of French bread. Small pieces of cooked sausages would make an alternative dipper for this fondue

SERVES 4

HIGHLAND FONDUE

A cheese fondue with a distinctly Scottish flavour.

YOU WILL NEED

15 g (½ oz) butter

1 small onion, finely chopped

250 ml (8 fl oz) milk

450 g (1 lb) mature Scottish Cheddar, grated

3 tsp cornflour

4 tbsp Scotch whisky

TO SERVE

Cubes of rye or whole meal bread

SERVES 4

1. Melt the butter in a saucepan over a low heat, add the onion and cook until soft, but not brown.

2. Add the milk and heat until bubbling. Gradually stir in the cheese and cook until the cheese has melted, stirring continuously.

3. In a small bowl, blend the cornflour with the whisky. Add to the cheese mixture, and continue to cook, stirring until thickened. Take care not to boil the fondue. Transfer to the fondue pot before bringing to the table. Serve with the cubes of rye or wholemeal bread for dipping.

DUTCH FONDUE

Holland has had a fondue tradition for a long time, using Dutch cheeses like Gouda or Edam flavoured with Dutch gin. If you do not want to use gin, try a little brandy or sherry instead. Very fresh, raw, whole button mushrooms, chunks of apple, celery sticks and rye bread would make a good alternative to crusty French bread for dipping.

1. Rub the inside of the fondue pot with the cut clove of garlic. Add the milk and heat until bubbling.

2. Gradually stir in the cheese and continue to heat, stirring all the time until the cheese has melted.

3. Add the fennel seeds. In a small bowl, blend the cornflour with the gin and then add to the cheese. Cook for another 2–3 minutes until smooth.

4. Transfer to the table and serve with mushrooms, apple, celery, and cubes of bread for dipping. Season with black pepper.

YOU WILL NEED

½ clove garlic

250 ml (8 fl oz) milk

450 g (1 lb) grated Gouda or Edam cheese

2 tsp fennel seeds

3 tsp cornflour

3 tbsp gin

freshly ground black pepper

TO SERVE

Button mushrooms, apple chunks, celery sticks and rye bread

SERVES 4

SMOKED CHEESE FONDUE

The strong flavour of smoked cheese means that you can make a fondue that is alcohol free. Emmental cheese is added to balance the flavour.

YOU WILL NEED

½ small onion

300 ml (10 fl oz) milk

300 g (10 oz) grated smoked cheese

100 g (4 oz) grated Emmental cheese

1 tbsp cornflour

TO SERVE

Crunchy apple, carrot sticks and rye bread

SERVES 4

1. Rub the inside of the fondue pot with the cut side of the onion. Put most of the milk into the pot, reserving 1–2 tbsp for later. Heat until gently bubbling.

2. Gradually add the cheeses and stir until melted, taking care not to boil the fondue.

3. Meanwhile, blend the cornflour with the reserved milk in a small bowl and add to the cheese mixture. Continue to cook for another 2–3 minutes until thickened. Serve with apple chunks, carrot sticks and cubes of rye bread.

THE STRONG FLAVOUR OF SMOKED CHEESE MEANS THAT YOU CAN MAKE A FONDUE THAT IS ALCOHOL FREE

ITALIAN THREE CHEESE FONDUE

Use one of the strong Italian cheeses like pecorino or Parmesan in this fondue to balance the flavour of the other milder, creamy Italian cheeses. For excellent flavour, buy the best mozzarella you can find, and grate the Parmesan or pecorino cheese yourself rather than buying it grated. To continue the Italian theme, try using cherry tomatoes and olives for dipping along with some crisp ciabatta bread, or grissini breadsticks.

1. Rub the inside of the fondue pot with the cut clove of garlic. Add the milk and heat until bubbling.

2. Gradually add all the cheeses and continue to heat gently until melted, stirring all the time.

3. Blend the cornflour with the white wine in a small bowl and add to the melted cheese. Continue to heat gently, stirring until thickened; do not allow to boil.

4. Transfer to the table and serve with the tomatoes, olives and breads for dipping.

YOU WILL NEED

½ clove garlic

300 ml (10 fl oz) milk

250 g (8 oz) mozzarella cheese, grated

250 g (8 oz) Dolcelatte cheese

50 g (2 oz) Parmesan or pecorino cheese, grated

2 tsp cornflour

3 tbsp dry white wine

TO SERVE

Cherry tomatoes, olives, ciabatta bread and breadsticks

SERVES 4

GREEK FONDUE

This is a substantial fondue using typically Greek ingredients. The best feta cheese to use is one that is made in Greece from sheep and goats' milk. Roasted red peppers are sold in tins or jars in large supermarkets or specialist delicatessens. Try using large peeled prawns to dip in the fondue, along with some cherry tomatoes and wedges of fresh fennel for an aromatic flavour. Strips of pitta bread would also be good here.

1. Put the wine, lemon juice and garlic in the fondue pot, and heat until simmering.

2. Gradually add the cheese, whisking in, and heat until melted. Take care not to boil the mixture.

3. Add the ouzo, olives, peppers, oregano or basil and feta, stirring well.

4. Transfer to the table and serve with the prawns, cherry tomatoes, and fennel chunks, together with some strips of pitta bread for dipping.

YOU WILL NEED

150 ml (5 fl oz) dry white wine

1 tbsp lemon juice

1 clove garlic, crushed

450 g (1 lb) Emmental cheese, grated

2 tbsp ouzo

50 g (2 oz) pitted black Kalamata olives in brine, drained and chopped

50 g (2 oz) roasted red pepper slices, drained and chopped

2 tsp fresh oregano or basil, chopped

2 oz (50 g) feta cheese, crumbled

TO SERVE

Large peeled prawns, cherry tomatoes, chunks of fennel and strips of pitta bread

SERVES 4

MEDITERRANEAN TOMATO FONDUE

This simple fondue is quickly made from store cupboard ingredients and makes an imaginative way to entertain impromptu guests. Keep some jars of the best-quality tomato pasta sauce in the cupboard for just such an occasion. Try serving some cubes of cooked chicken to dip in this rich sauce.

YOU WILL NEED

½ clove garlic

790 g (28 oz) jar of tomato pasta sauce

350 g (12 oz) mozzarella cheese, roughly chopped

150 ml (5 fl oz) red wine

a handful of fresh basil leaves

2–3 tbsp Parmesan cheese, freshly grated

TO SERVE

Cubes of ciabatta bread, olives, celery sticks, pieces of cooked chicken

SERVES 4-6

1. Rub the inside of the fondue pot with the cut clove of garlic. Add the pasta sauce, mozzarella cheese and red wine, put over a medium heat, and cook gently until the cheese is melted.

2. Transfer to the table and, sprinkle the fondue with basil leaves and grated Parmesan cheese. Serve with bread cubes, olives, etc. for dipping.

- *To make the chicken dippers, cut up one or two chicken breasts into chunks or strips, and fry in olive oil until brown. Cool, cover and keep in the refrigerator until needed.*

THE **CLASSIC**
COMBINATION
OF CHEESE AND
BACON WORKS
PERFECTLY IN **FONDUE**

CHEESE AND BACON FONDUE

The classic combination of cheese and bacon works perfectly in fondue. cherry tomato dippers cut through the creamy richness of this recipe beautifully.

1. Put the oil into a deep saucepan over a medium heat and fry the bacon until crisp. Remove and set aside to cool.

2. Add the onion, garlic and mushrooms to the pan, and cook gently for 4–5 minutes, taking care not to burn the garlic.

3. Sprinkle over the cornflour, and mix well with a wooden spoon. Gradually add the milk, mixing until smooth. Slowly add the cheese, stirring constantly until melted. If the fondue is too thick add a little extra hot milk.

4. Add the Worcestershire sauce, mustard powder, and hot pepper sauce, and most of the bacon, reserving a little for garnish.

5. Transfer to the fondue pot and take to the table to keep warm. Serve with cubes of bread for dipping.

YOU WILL NEED

2 tbsp vegetable oil

5 slices bacon, chopped

I onion, finely chopped

I clove garlic, crushed

100 g (4 oz) button mushrooms, finely sliced

I tbsp cornflour

300 ml (10 fl oz) milk

675 g (1 ½ lb) mature Cheddar, grated

I tsp Worcestershire sauce

I tsp mustard powder

I tsp hot pepper sauce

TO SERVE

Cubes of crusty bread, cherry tomatoes

SERVES 4–6

ISRAELI FONDUE

An unusual fondue using rich avocados, creamy Edam cheese, and sour cream or crème fraîche. Serve with spicy accompaniments like chunks of red and yellow peppers, pieces of salami, as well as tomatoes, and possibly large peeled prawns. For a bread dipper, try some toasted seed or granary bread for a crunchy texture. Prepare the fondue at the very last minute to prevent it discolouring.

YOU WILL NEED

½ clove garlic

175 ml (6 fl oz) dry white wine

350 g (12 oz) Edam cheese, grated

2 large ripe avocados

2 tsp lemon juice

2 tsp cornflour

150 ml (5 fl oz) sour cream or crème fraîche

black pepper

TO SERVE

Red and yellow peppers, salami, tomatoes, large peeled prawns, cubes of toasted seed or granary bread

SERVES 4

1. Rub the inside of the fondue pot with the cut clove of garlic. Pour in the wine and heat until simmering.

2. Lower the heat and gradually stir in the cheese, stir constantly and continue to cook until melted. Remove from the heat while you prepare the avocados.

3. Halve the avocados, remove the stones and scoop out the flesh into a bowl. Add the lemon juice and mash until smooth.

4. Blend the cornflour with the sour cream or crème fraîche in a small bowl. Add to the cheese mixture with the mashed avocado, mix well and continue to cook, stirring continuously for another four or five minutes until thickened. Take care not to boil the mixture. Season with black pepper and transfer to the table.

5. Serve with chunks of peppers, salami, tomatoes, prawns and cubes of toasted bread for dipping.

ITALY HAS ANOTHER VERSION OF FONDUE USING FONTINA CHEESE AND ITALIAN WHITE VERMOUTH

FONDUTA

Italy has another version of fondue using fontina cheese and Italian white vermouth. Serve with breadsticks to swirl around in the cheese. If you cannot get fontina cheese, try using Gruyère instead.

YOU WILL NEED

250 ml (8 fl oz) Italian white vermouth
450 g (1 lb) fontina cheese, grated
2 tsp cornflour
2 egg yolks
250 ml (8 fl oz) dry white wine
a few drops of hot pepper sauce
ground white pepper and salt

TO SERVE

Grissini breadsticks

SERVES 4

1. Put the vermouth in the fondue pot and bring to a gentle simmer over a low heat. Gradually add the cheese, stirring all the time until the cheese is melted.

2. Blend the cornflour with the egg yolks and a little of the white wine to form a smooth mixture. Add to the melted cheese with the rest of the wine, and continue to cook until thickened, stirring constantly. Do not allow to boil.

3. Transfer to the table and serve with breadsticks for dipping.

4. Add salt and pepper and a few drops of hot pepper sauce to taste.

NORMANDY FONDUE

Camembert is a superb cheese for making fondues. If your Camembert is really ripe and already runny, it is almost a fondue in itself. Here Camembert is combined with Calvados, the wonderfully pungent apple brandy from Normandy, France. Use ordinary brandy if you do not have Calvados.

YOU WILL NEED

½ clove garlic

250 ml (8 fl oz) dry white wine

150 ml (5 fl oz) crème fraîche

300 g (10 oz) ripe Camembert, rind removed, and chopped

2 tsp cornflour

1 tbsp lemon juice

3 tbsp Calvados or brandy

TO SERVE

Chunks of crisp apple, celery sticks and cubes of fried bread

SERVES 4

1. Rub the inside of the fondue pot with the cut clove of garlic. Pour in the wine and bring to a gentle simmer over a low heat.

2. Add the crème fraîche and Camembert cheese, and continue to cook until the cheese is melted, stirring all the time.

3. Mix the cornflour with the lemon juice and the Calvados. Add to the cheese mixture and continue to cook until thickened.

4. Serve with apple chunks, celery sticks and cubes of fried bread for dipping.

- *To make fried bread for dipping, cut some day-old white bread into cubes about 2.5 cm (1 in.) across. Fry quickly in olive oil. Alternatively, you can toss the bread cubes in olive oil and bake on a tray in the oven at 180°C (350°F) for ten minutes.*

- •• *Tip: put the Camembert into the freezer for thirty minutes before cutting off the rind.*

BAKED CAMEMBERT FONDUE

This is a great idea for a dinner party, where you could serve this as the cheese course between the main course and the dessert, or at the end of the meal. It also makes a superb addition to a buffet. You do not need a fondue pot as the Camembert cheese is baked and served in the box on the table. For dipping just use grissini breadsticks. Allow one Camembert for every four people.

YOU WILL NEED

1 Camembert cheese in a wooden box

TO SERVE

Grissini breadsticks

SERVES 4

1. Heat the oven to 180°C (350°F).

2. Remove the Camembert cheese from its box and its wrapping. Keep the base of the box for serving.

3. Wrap the cheese in a sheet of tin foil and put onto a baking tray. Cook in the oven for 10–15 minutes.

4. Remove the tray from the oven, and allow to cool for a minute or two. Open the foil and cut a large cross in the centre of the cheese to open the crust and reveal the gooey inside. Place into the base of the wooden box.

5. Serve immediately with breadsticks for dipping.

BRIE WITH RED ONION FONDUE

Red onions are pretty as well as being mild and sweet. Here they are caramelised in balsamic vinegar. This gives a lovely sharpness to balance the creaminess of the Brie. Slice the onions into very thin rings so that they can be picked up easily on the dippers. Use blanched French beans and asparagus, raw courgette sticks, tiny boiled new potatoes for dipping and you have the perfect summer fondue.

1. Melt the butter in a small, heavy pan over a low heat. Add the onions, cover and cook very gently for 15 minutes, stirring from time to time. Do not allow to brown. Remove the cover, sprinkle over the sugar, raise the heat, and cook for another 2–3 minutes until caramelised. Add the vinegar and thyme, and cook until the liquid has evaporated. Set aside to cool.

2. Sprinkle the cornflour over the Brie. Put the wine, lemon juice, and garlic into the fondue pot over a medium heat and bring to a low simmer. Gradually add the cheese and continue to cook, stirring all the time until the cheese is melted. Sprinkle the caramelised onions on top.

3. Transfer to the table and serve with the vegetables and bread cubes.

YOU WILL NEED

50 g (2 oz) butter

2 small red onions, thinly sliced

1 tsp sugar

2 tsp balsamic vinegar

1 tsp chopped fresh thyme

1 tbsp cornflour

450 g (1 lb) Brie cheese, rind removed and cut into cubes

150 ml (5 fl oz) dry white wine

1 tbsp lemon juice

1 clove garlic, crushed

TO SERVE

Blanched French beans and asparagus spears, raw courgette sticks, tiny boiled new potatoes or cubes of crusty bread

SERVES 4

• *Tip: put the Brie into the freezer for thirty minutes before cutting off the rind.*

COMBINE A CREAMY, MILD CREAM CHEESE **WITH** A GOOD **BLUE** STILTON CHEESE TO GIVE A WELL-**BALANCED** FLAVOUR

BLUE CHEESE FONDUE

Combine a creamy, mild cream cheese
with a good blue stilton cheese to give a
well-balanced flavour, and serve with crusty
bread and celery sticks.

1. Put the milk and cream cheese into the fondue pot and, using
a whisk, beat until creamy. Put over a gentle heat and gradually
stir in the blue cheese. Continue to heat, stirring constantly to
make a smooth mixture.

2. Blend the cornflour with the cream in a small bowl. Stir into the
cheese mixture and cook for another 2–3 minutes until thick and
creamy. Serve with cubes of bread and celery sticks
for dipping.

YOU WILL NEED

250 ml (8 fl oz) milk

225 g (8 oz) cream cheese

225 g (8 oz) blue Stilton cheese, grated

3 tsp cornflour

2 tbsp single cream

TO SERVE

Cubes of crusty bread and celery sticks

SERVES 4

FISH FONDUE

CONTENTS

BAGNA CAUDA FONDUE

This lovely Italian dish is a real classic. It is more a warm dip than a true fondue, but it is usually cooked on the table in a small terra cotta pot set over a candle burner so fits the bill perfectly. Bagna Cauda, rich with the flavours of garlic, anchovy and olive oil, is often served with a selection of young summer vegetables (for dipping.) Try fresh radishes, cherry tomatoes, spring onions, baby carrots, sticks of fennel, celery or cucumber. It is also good with pieces of lightly toasted pitta bread or cubes of feta cheese.

YOU WILL NEED

50 g (2 oz) unsalted butter

100 ml (3 fl oz) extra virgin olive oil

3–4 cloves garlic, crushed

25 g (1 oz) anchovies packed in olive oil

3–4 tbsp double cream

TO SERVE

Summer vegetables, toasted pitta bread, cubes of feta cheese

SERVES 4

1. Put the butter, olive oil, and garlic in the fondue pot (a terra cotta one with a candle burner is ideal). Warm until the butter is melted, making sure that the butter and garlic do not burn.

2. Drain and chop the anchovies, reserving a little of their oil. Add the anchovies and a little of the reserved oil to the butter mixture. Continue to cook for four or five minutes, stirring with a wooden spoon, crushing the anchovies and the garlic to make a smoother consistency.

3. Stir in the cream and serve with the vegetables, pitta bread, and feta cheese for dipping.

SEAFOOD HOTPOT FONDUE

This is based on a traditional Szechuan style of hotpot, and the seafood is cooked in a flavoured stock. This is a perfect way to cook seafood as it doesn't take long to cook and is much tastier if it isn't overcooked. Cooking like this means that it is easy to get the timing just right. After you have cooked the pieces of seafood in the stock, dip them in a sauce for extra zing.

1. Put the stock in the fondue pot with the red chilli, fish or soy sauce, sherry and garlic, and bring to a gentle simmer over a medium heat. Continue cooking gently for 4–5 minutes to allow the flavours to develop.

2. Meanwhile, lay out the fish and seafood on a plate ready to cook together with the sauce or salsa. Transfer the fondue pot to the table.

3. Cook the raw fish and seafood first, then the cooked fish. You can hold individual pieces in the stock with skewers or chopsticks. Alternatively, you can plunge everything in the stock, leaving it to cook, and then remove using a draining spoon or small sieve. The mussels will be cooked when the shells open. Serve the cooked fish and seafood with the sauce.

4. If you would like to make the stock into a more substantial soup, add the rice or noodles to the fondue pot and cook for ten minutes until soft. Serve this as a soup after the fish. Alternatively, simply dunk pieces of crusty bread into the stock to mop up the wonderful flavours, and eat with the fish and seafood.

WARNING: after cooking, any unopened shellfish should be thrown away and not opened, or eaten.

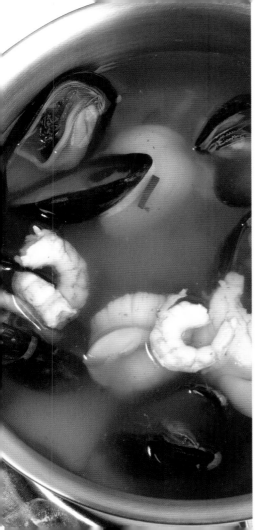

YOU WILL NEED

For the stock:

600 ml (20 fl oz) fish stock

1 red chilli, de-seeded and finely chopped

1–2 tbsp fish sauce or soy sauce

1 tbsp dry sherry

2 cloves garlic, finely chopped

For the seafood:

2 lemon sole fillets, cut into strips

8–12 large shrimp, ready cooked

8 large scallops

8 large mussels, in their shells, trimmed and scrubbed

50 g (2 oz) quick-cook long grain rice or noodles (optional)

TO SERVE

Cubes of crusty bread

SERVES 4

DEEP FRIED FISH FONDUE

Little pieces of fish and seafood are coated in a light batter and then fried in a hot oil fondue. Serve with lemon quarters, Tarragon Sauce (p. 87), Garlic Sauce (p. 88), or mayonnaise. For an even easier dish, use ready-coated frozen fish and seafood.

YOU WILL NEED

For the seafood:

450 g (1½ lb) mixed fish and seafood (salmon, monkfish, whitebait, squid rings, large prawns or fleshy white fish) cornflour, for dusting fish

For the batter:

225 g (8 oz) plain flour

pinch salt

300 ml (10 fl oz) water

1 tbsp olive oil

2 eggs, separated

vegetable oil for frying

TO SERVE

Lemon quarters, Tarragon Sauce (p. 87), Garlic Sauce (p. 88), mayonnaise

1. Cut the fish into small pieces, 2.5–3.5 cm (1–1½ in.) long. Arrange everything on a plate and dust with cornflour.

2. Make the batter by sifting the flour and salt into a bowl. Make a well in the centre and add the water, olive oil and egg yolks. Beat well using an electric whisk.

3. In a separate bowl, whisk the egg whites until stiff, and fold into the flour mixture using a metal spoon.

4. Half fill the fondue pot with oil and heat on the cooker to 190°C (375°F), or until a cube of bread dropped into the oil browns in 30 seconds. Transfer the pot to the table burner, making sure it is very stable.

5. Each person then spears some fish, dips it in the batter and cooks it in the hot oil until crisp and golden. Serve with your choice of dips.

SICILIAN TUNA FONDUE

The very best tomato fondue is used here to cook tuna and Mediterranean vegetables.

1. Cut the tuna steak into chunks and place on a serving plate with the peppers.

2. Put the olive oil and butter into a pan over a low heat. When the butter has melted, add the onion and garlic and cook for 5–10 minutes until very soft but not brown.

3. Add the passata, oregano, sugar, salt, and pepper and cook over a low heat for 15–20 minutes, covering the pan and stirring from time to time.

4. Add the milk and stir to mix, cooking for another 2–3 minutes. Pour into the fondue pot and transfer to the table burner.

5. Each person spears a piece of tuna and pepper and cooks them in the tomato sauce. Serve with the potatoes and salad. When all the tuna and peppers have been cooked, serve the rest of the tomato sauce, perhaps with some warm bread for dunking.

TO SERVE

Potatoes roasted in olive oil and a crunchy salad

SERVES 4

YOU WILL NEED

450 g (1 lb) fresh tuna steak

1 red, 1 yellow and 1 green pepper, cut into small chunks

1 tbsp olive oil

25 g (1 oz) butter

1 onion, finely chopped

3 cloves garlic, crushed

560 g (1 lb 4 oz) jar of passata (sieved tomatoes)

1 tsp dried oregano

1 tsp sugar

salt and freshly ground black pepper

75 ml (3 fl oz) milk

VEGETABLE FONDUE

CONTENTS

VEGETABLE HOTPOT FONDUE

Serve this vegetable fondue with potatoes and cherry tomatoes, and fried bread crostinis made by frying thin slices of French bread in olive oil until crisp and golden.

1. Chop all the vegetables finely and put into a saucepan with the stock and mixed herbs. Bring to the boil and simmer gently until tender. Drain the vegetables, reserving the liquid, and leave to cool slightly.

2. Purée the vegetables in a blender or food processor and then rub the purée through a sieve into the fondue pot. Put the pot over a low heat and add the butter, beating well. Season with salt, pepper and nutmeg. Add a dash of the reserved liquid if the purée seems a little thick.

3. Transfer to the table burner and serve with the potatoes, cherry tomatoes and fried bread crostinis for dipping.

YOU WILL NEED

1 small onion

225 g (8 oz) carrots

1 small turnip

½ small rutabaga

300 ml (10 fl oz) vegetable stock (made from vegetable bouillon powder or stock concentrate)

1 tsp dried mixed herbs

50 g (2 oz) butter, diced

salt and freshly ground black pepper

pinch freshly grated nutmeg

TO SERVE

Small new potatoes, cherry tomatoes, fried bread crostinis

SERVES 4

A PERFECT WINTER WARMER AND A GREAT ALTERNATIVE TO SOUP

LEEK FONDUE

A perfect winter warmer and a great alternative to soup.

YOU WILL NEED

900 g (2 lb) leeks

2 tbsp olive oil

150 ml (5 fl oz) vegetable stock (made from vegetable bouillon powder or stock concentrate)

50 g (2 oz) butter

salt and freshly ground black pepper

pinch of freshly grated nutmeg

2 spring onions, chopped

small bunch fresh chives, snipped

TO SERVE

Raw cauliflower florets, carrot sticks, button mushrooms and cubes of toasted rye bread

SERVES 4

1. Trim the leeks, wash well, and chop coarsely. Put the olive oil into a saucepan over a low heat. Add the leeks and cook very slowly for 10–15 minutes until soft but not brown. If they start to stick, add a little water. Remove from heat and allow to cool slightly.

2. Process the leeks in a food processor or blender with the stock until smooth. Put into the fondue pot. Place over a low heat and beat in the butter. Season with salt, pepper and nutmeg. Stir in the spring onions and chives, and transfer to the table burner.

3. Serve with the raw vegetables and rye bread for dipping.

MUSHROOM FONDUE

This creamy fondue is lovely served with cubes of a crumbly cheese like Cheshire or Lancashire, some celery sticks and chunks of crusty French bread for dipping. Use the freshest mushrooms you can find.

YOU WILL NEED

50 g (2 oz) butter

450 g (1 lb) mushrooms, thinly sliced

2 cloves garlic, crushed

½ tsp dried thyme, or a sprig of fresh thyme

150 ml (5 fl oz) vegetable stock (made from vegetable bouillon powder or stock concentrate)

150 ml (5 fl oz) double cream

1–2 tsp cornflour

pinch cayenne pepper

dash of Worcestershire sauce

salt and freshly ground black pepper

2 tbsp chopped fresh parsley

TO SERVE

Cubes of cheese – Cheshire or Lancashire, celery sticks and French bread

1. Melt the butter in a saucepan over a low heat. Add the mushrooms, garlic and thyme, and cook very gently for ten minutes. Add the stock and simmer for ten minutes. Cool slightly and then purée in a blender or processor.

2. Put a little cream into the fondue pot, add the cornflour and mix to a smooth paste. Add the rest of the cream and the mushroom purée. Bring to a low simmer and cook until thickened, stirring all the time. Add the cayenne pepper and the Worcestershire sauce. Season with salt and pepper and stir in the parsley.

3. Transfer to the table burner and serve with cubes of cheese, celery sticks and cubes of French bread for dipping.

SERVES 4

MEAT FONDUE

CONTENTS

FONDUE BOURGUIGNONNE

In this simple fondue, tender pieces of fillet steak are deep fried in hot oil at the table. The succulent pieces of meat are then dipped in one of a selection of sauces. Try serving Pesto Dip (p. 94) and Easy Tomato Sauce (p. 91) for contrast in flavours and colours, together with Horseradish Sauce (p. 95). Also serve with a basket of crusty French bread and a green salad.

1. Cut the steak into 2.5 cm (1 in.) cubes and put on a serving dish.

2. Put enough oil into a fondue pot to half fill it. Heat on the cooker to 190°C (375°F), or until a cube of bread dropped into the oil browns in thirty seconds. Transfer the pot to the table burner, making sure it is very stable.

3. Each person then spears a piece of steak and cooks it in the oil. After dipping in a sauce, the pieces are eaten with a knife and fork with the bread and salad.

YOU WILL NEED

1 kg (2 lb) fillet steak

Vegetable oil for frying

TO SERVE

Pesto Dip and Tomato Sauce for a contrast in flavours, Horseradish Sauce, a basket of crusty French bread and a green salad

SERVES 4

MIDDLE EASTERN LAMB FONDUE

Marinate chunks of lamb fillet in lemon juice, garlic, oregano and rosemary before plunging into hot oil to cook, and you will have a most delicious aromatic result.

1. Cut the lamb fillet into chunks 2.5 cm (1 in.) across. Put into a bowl with the lemon juice, crushed garlic, oregano, and rosemary. Season with black pepper and toss in the olive oil. Cover and put in the fridge to marinate for one to eight hours before cooking. After marinating, remove the lamb from the marinade, and pat dry with a piece of kitchen towel. Put onto a serving plate.

2. Put enough oil into a fondue pot to half fill it. Heat on the cooker to 190°C (375°F), or until a cube of bread dropped into the oil browns in thirty seconds. Transfer the pot to the table burner, making sure it is very stable.

3. Each person then spears a piece of lamb and cooks it in the oil. The pieces are eaten with a knife and fork with the sauces, bread and salad.

YOU WILL NEED

1 kg (2 lb) lamb fillet
juice of 2 lemons
2 cloves garlic, crushed
1 tsp dried oregano
a few leaves of fresh rosemary
freshly ground black pepper
2 tbsp olive oil
vegetable oil for frying

TO SERVE

Tzatziki (p. 93), Apricot Relish (p. 92), pitta bread, and a salad of tomatoes, peppers, cucumber and olives

SERVES 4

MINCED LAMB FONDUE

Tasty little meatballs are here cooked in a hot oil fondue. Serve with Simple Mushroom Sauce (p. 86) and perhaps a dish of creamy mashed potatoes.

1. Put all the ingredients for the meatballs into a large bowl. Season and mix together well. Using damp hands, shape the mixture into 20–24 balls, each the size of a walnut. Put on a plate, cover and put in the fridge for at least one hour.

2. Half fill a fondue pot with oil and heat on the cooker to 190°C (375°F), or until a cube of bread dropped into the oil browns in thirty seconds. Transfer the pot to the table burner, making sure it is very stable.

3. Warm the mushroom sauce and put on the table with other accompaniments.

4. Each person then spears a meatball and cooks it in the oil. They are then eaten with a knife and fork with the sauce, and other accompaniments.

YOU WILL NEED

600 g (1lb 4 oz) lean lamb mince

3 spring onions, finely chopped

50 g (2 oz) fresh breadcrumbs

2 tbsp Parmesan cheese, freshly grated

2 tsp dried oregano

2 tbsp fresh parsley, chopped

salt and black pepper

vegetable oil for frying

TO SERVE

Mushroom sauce and creamy mashed potatoes

SERVES 4

TARRAGON CHICKEN FONDUE

Chicken breast is succulent cooked like this, and is a perfect match with the slightly pungent flavour of tarragon. Fresh tarragon is best and is easily available in big supermarkets. You could substitute dried tarragon or try fresh coriander for a different slant.

1. Prepare the accompanying sauce(s). Cut the chicken into thin strips or small chunks as you prefer, and arrange on a serving dish. Use a separate dish for the carrots, cauliflower and courgette.

2. Put the wine, chicken stock, onion, garlic and tarragon into the fondue pot. Bring to a gentle boil and simmer for 4–5 minutes to allow the flavours to develop.

3. Spear pieces of chicken and vegetables on a fondue fork and cook in the bubbling stock. Vegetables take 1–2 minutes, chicken 3–4 minutes. Make sure the chicken is no longer pink. Do not add too many pieces of food at once to the stock.

4. Dip the cooked vegetables and chicken into the sauces.

YOU WILL NEED

450 g (1 lb) skinless, boneless chicken breasts

2 medium carrots, cut on the slant into thin slices

1 small cauliflower, cut into small florets

2 small courgette, cut into thin slices

300 ml (10 fl oz) dry white wine

300 ml (10 fl oz) chicken stock (homemade or made with stock concentrate if possible)

1 small onion, finely sliced

1 clove garlic, crushed

1 tbsp fresh tarragon, snipped or 1 tsp dried tarragon

TO SERVE

Tarragon dipping sauce (p. 87) or ready-made salsa

SERVES 4

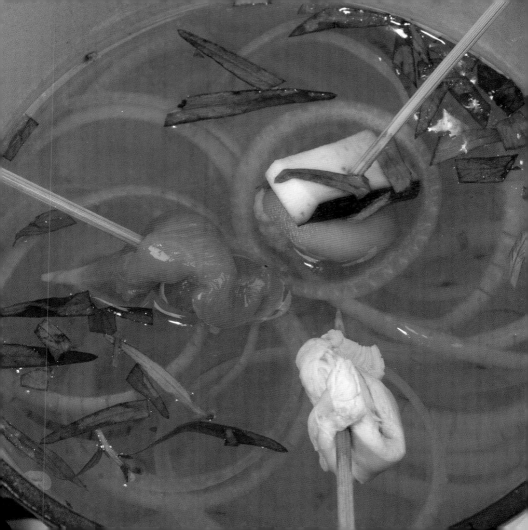

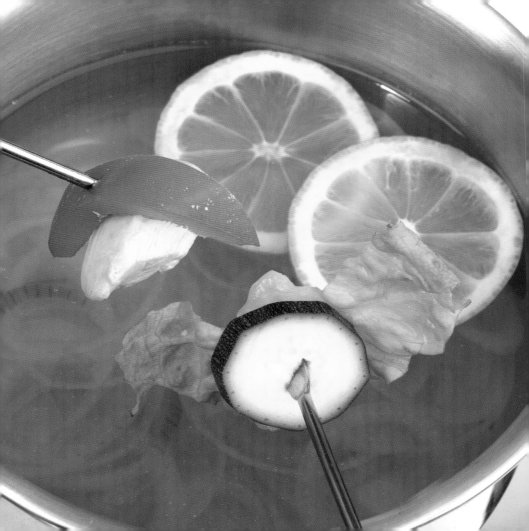

ORIENTAL GINGER CHICKEN

Serve this spicy chicken Mongolian-style Hot Pot
with Garlic Sauce (p. 88) and Hot Chilli Sauce (p. 89)

1. Prepare the accompanying sauces. Cut the chicken into thin strips
or small chunks, and arrange on a serving dish. Arrange the
broccoli, courgette, pepper, lettuce leaves and mushrooms.

2. Put the wine, chicken stock, onion, garlic, lemon slices, ginger,
sugar and soy sauce into the fondue pot. Bring to a gentle boil and
simmer for 4–5 minutes to allow the flavours to develop.

3. Spear pieces of chicken and vegetables on a fondue fork and
cook in the bubbling stock. Vegetables take 1–2 minutes, chicken
3–4 minutes. Make sure the chicken is no longer pink. Do not add
too many pieces of food at once to the stock.

4. Dip the cooked vegetables and chicken into the sauces and eat.

YOU WILL NEED

450 g (1 lb) skinless, boneless chicken breasts

100 g (4 oz) broccoli, cut into florets

2 small courgette, thinly sliced

1 red or yellow pepper, cut into thin strips

A few torn leaves of Romaine or gem lettuce

100 g (4 oz) very fresh small button mushrooms

300 ml (10 fl oz) dry white wine

300 ml (10 fl oz) chicken stock (homemade or
made with stock concentrate)

1 small onion, finely sliced

1 clove garlic, crushed

2 slices lemon

2 tbsp fresh ginger, peeled and very
finely chopped

2 tsp sugar

1 tsp soy sauce

TO SERVE

Garlic Sauce (p. 88) and Hot Chilli Sauce (p. 89)

SERVES 4

CRISPY SAUSAGE BITES

These crispy little sausage meatballs are delicious served with Sweet Tomato Relish (p. 90) or with Easy Tomato Sauce (p. 91). A crisp green salad is the perfect accompaniment. Choose a sausage meat with a very high meat content for the best flavour.

1. Put the sausage meat and onion into a frying pan and cook over a medium heat until brown and crumbly. Turn into a large bowl, and allow to cool for a few minutes.

2. Add the cream cheese, parsley, mustard, fresh breadcrumbs and salt and pepper. Mix well and, using your hands, form into 16–20 small balls.

3. Dip each ball first in beaten egg and then dry breadcrumbs. Put into the fridge to chill for at least an hour.

4. Prepare the sauces.

5. Half fill a fondue pot with oil and heat on the cooker to 190°C (375°F), or until a cube of bread dropped into the oil browns in thirty seconds. Transfer the pot to the table burner, making sure it is very stable.

6. Each person then spears a sausage ball, cooks it in the oil until crisp and golden, and then dips it in a sauce before eating.

YOU WILL NEED

450 g (1 lb) best quality sausage meat

1 small onion, finely chopped

50 g (2 oz) cream cheese

1 tbsp fresh parsley, chopped

1 tsp Dijon mustard

2 tbsp fresh breadcrumbs

salt and freshly ground black pepper

2 eggs, beaten

75 g (3 oz) dry breadcrumbs

vegetable oil for frying

TO SERVE

Sweet Tomato Relish (p. 90), Easy Tomato Sauce (p. 91), and a green salad

SERVES 4

SIMPLE MUSHROOM SAUCE

This simple sauce goes well
with a lamb or chicken fondue
and turns simply-cooked meat
into a complete dish.

YOU WILL NEED

50 g (2 oz) butter

150 g (6 oz) button mushrooms, finely chopped

1 tsp dried thyme

1½ tbsp plain flour

300 ml (10 fl oz) milk

1 tbsp dry sherry

salt and pepper

1. Melt the butter in a saucepan over a low heat. Add the
mushrooms and thyme and cook gently for 5–10 minutes until the
mushrooms are very soft and have released their juice.

2. Sprinkle over the flour, and cook for a minute or two. Gradually
stir in the milk, and bring to the boil, stirring all the time to thicken
the sauce. Add the sherry and season with salt and pepper.
Serve warm.

TARRAGON
DIPPING SAUCE

This sauce is quick to make and goes well with any fondue, especially chicken and fish.

1. Mix all the ingredients together in a bowl. Cover and keep in the refrigerator until needed.

2. Serve cold or warm. To serve warm, put into a heatproof bowl over a pan of simmering water and heat gently, stirring all the time.

YOU WILL NEED

3 tbsp mayonnaise

3 tbsp thick yoghurt (not low fat)

1 tbsp extra virgin olive oil

1 tsp Dijon mustard

½ tsp honey

1 tbsp fresh tarragon, snipped

GARLIC SAUCE

A simple garlic sauce for those who can't get enough of this pungent bulb.

Combine all the ingredients together in a small bowl, cover and keep in the refrigerator until needed.

YOU WILL NEED

150 ml (5 fl oz) thick Greek yoghurt or crème fraîche

2 cloves garlic, crushed

2 tsp dried mint

salt and freshly ground black pepper

HOT CHILLI
SAUCE

Good to give an extra kick to
most meat fondues.

Put all the ingredients together in a screw-top jar.
Keep in the refrigerator until needed. Shake well before
putting into a small bowl for serving.

YOU WILL NEED

75 ml (3 fl oz) extra virgin olive oil

2 tbsp lime or lemon juice

1 tbsp soy sauce

1 tsp sugar

1 small red chilli, de-seeded and very finely chopped

SWEET TOMATO RELISH

Serve with Crispy Sausage Bites (p. 84),
or with Deep Fried Fish Fondue (p. 61)

1. Heat the oil in a pan over a medium heat and add
the onion and garlic. Cook for 4–5 minutes
until very soft.

2. Add the tomatoes and tomato pureé to the pan.
Cook gently for 15–20 minutes, stirring from time to
time until the sauce is thick and reduced.

3. Stir in the pickle relish and parsley and serve warm.

YOU WILL NEED

1 tbsp olive oil
1 small onion, finely chopped
1 clove garlic, crushed
400 g (14 oz) tin chopped tomatoes
2 tbsp tomato pureé
2 tbsp sweet pickle relish
2 tbsp chopped fresh parsley

EASY **TOMATO** SAUCE

Lovely with Crispy Sausage Bites (p. 84) or Minced Lamb Fondue (p. 79).

1. Put the olive oil into a pan over a low heat, add the onion and garlic and cook for 5–10 minutes until very soft but not brown.

2. Add the tomatoes, oregano, sugar, salt and pepper and cook over a low heat for 15–20 minutes, covering the pan and stirring from time to time.

3. Add the milk and stir to mix, cooking for another 2–3 minutes. Serve warm.

YOU WILL NEED

1 tbsp olive oil
1 onion, finely chopped
1 clove garlic, crushed
400 g (14 oz) tin chopped tomatoes
1 tbsp fresh oregano, chopped
1 tsp sugar
salt and freshly ground black pepper
75 ml (3 fl oz) milk

APRICOT RELISH

Perfect with Middle Eastern Lamb Fondue (p. 76)

1. Heat the oil in a saucepan, add the onion and garlic and cook over a low heat until soft.

2. Add the apricots and juice and the sherry and simmer for five minutes. Purée in a blender or food processor, season with salt and pepper and stir in the lemon juice and parsley. Serve warm.

YOU WILL NEED

1 tbsp olive oil
1 small onion, finely chopped
1 clove garlic, crushed
400 g (14 oz) tin apricots in natural juice, not syrup
1 tsp dry sherry
salt and freshly ground black pepper
1 tbsp lemon juice
2 tbsp parsley, finely chopped

CONTENTS

There is something undeniably extravagant about sweet fondues. They can be simple yet quite luxurious – think plump strawberries dipped into silky, dark, melted chocolate, amaretti biscuits dunked in a rich toffee fondue, puff pastry twists with warm summer fruits. A sweet fondue can obviously be served after a main course fondue, but it can also make a fun dessert after a more traditional meal. There are ideas here for different sweet fondues and on pages 120-127 there are recipes for dipping accompaniments.

SIMPLY CHOCOLATE

Choose the best chocolate for this simple fondue. The chocolate is melted with double cream, so a dark, plain chocolate is best. Choose one that contains 50–75 per cent cocoa solids – any higher than this, and the chocolate can be a little unstable when melted and may split. This type of fondue works very well with a terra cotta fondue pot with a built-in candle burner. This gives a gentle heat which will not burn the chocolate or cream.

Break up the chocolate into the fondue pot. Add the cream and heat gently, stirring all the time until the chocolate is melted. Serve with fruit and other accompaniments for dipping.

- To make Chocolate Orange Fondue, follow the above recipe, adding two tablespoons of orange liqueur once the chocolate has melted. A little grated orange peel could also be substituted for a non-alcoholic version.

YOU WILL NEED

340 g (12 oz) plain chocolate (50–75% cocoa solids)

300 ml (10 fl oz) double cream

TO SERVE

Fresh fruit – strawberries, pineapple chunks, peach slices, grapes, etc. Meringue Fingers, (see p. 124) amaretti biscuits or sponge fingers

SERVES 4

CRÈME CARAMEL FONDUE

A creamy caramel-swirled fondue to serve with Puff Pastry Twists (p. 125).

1. Put the sugar into a heavy saucepan over a moderate heat. Cook until the sugar melts and turns golden brown. Do not stir the sugar as it will crystalise, simply swirl the pan a little as the sugar is melting. When the sugar has melted and turned golden brown, remove from the heat and immediately add the water, stirring in with a spoon to mix well. Set aside to cool.

2. Put the custard, cream and vanilla extract into the fondue pot over a low heat and bring to a low simmer. Stir in the caramel sauce until it is swirled through the custard, but not completely mixed.

YOU WILL NEED

75 g (3 oz) sugar

3 tbsp water

425 g (15 oz) tin ready-made custard

300 ml (10 fl oz) double cream

1 tsp vanilla extract

TO SERVE

Puff Pastry Twists (p. 125)

SERVES 4

BLACK CHERRY FONDUE

Another simple fondue made from store cupboard ingredients.

1. Put the cherry conserve into the fondue pot over a moderate heat, add the lemon juice, and warm until the conserve has become liquid.

2. Add the custard and milk and continue to heat, stirring well for another 4–5 minutes. Serve with Meringue Fingers (p. 124) and shortbread for dipping.

YOU WILL NEED

350 g (12 oz) jar black cherry conserve

Juice of half a lemon

425 g (15 oz) tin ready-made custard

150 ml (5 fl oz) milk

TO SERVE

Meringue Fingers (p. 124) and shortbread

SERVES 4

CARAMEL AND NOUGAT FONDUE

A fun fondue which has a rich toffee flavour. Serve
with Frozen Bananas (p. 122) to add to the fun.

Chop the chocolate bars into small chunks. Put into the fondue pot with the cream
over a low heat. Heat very gently, stirring constantly until the pieces have melted.

YOU WILL NEED

4 standard sized, caramel and nougat chocolate bars

150 ml (5 fl oz) single cream

TO SERVE

Frozen Bananas

SERVES 4

WHITE CHOCOLATE BRANDY FONDUE

Brandy gives a subtle kick to this otherwise rich
mixture of white chocolate and cream.
Serve with chunks of sharp fruit such as kiwi,
pear or apple.

Break up the chocolate and put into the fondue pot with the cream.
Melt over a gentle heat, stirring all the time until the chocolate is
melted. Stir in the brandy. Serve with the fruit for dipping.

YOU WILL NEED

200 g (7 oz) white chocolate

1 ½ tbsp brandy

25 g (1 oz) unsalted butter

2 tbsp Greek yoghurt or crème fraîche

150 ml (5 fl oz) double cream

TO SERVE

Serve with chunks of sharp fruit such as kiwi,
pear or apple

SERVES 4

MOCHA FONDUE

Dunk crisp Puff Pastry Twists (p.125) and chunks of fresh pineapple into this coffee-flavoured chocolate sensation. Add the Irish cream liqueur for an extra kick.

Break up the chocolate into the fondue pot, add the cream, put over a low heat and cook until the chocolate has melted, stirring all the time. Add the coffee liquid and the liqueur, if desired.

YOU WILL NEED

225 g (8 oz) plain chocolate

150 ml (5 fl oz) double cream

1 tbsp instant coffee granules dissolved in 1 tbsp hot water

3 tbsp Irish cream liqueur (optional)

TO SERVE

Puff Pastry Twists and fresh pineapple

SERVES 4

SUMMER FRUIT FONDUE

Use a selection of summer fruits – raspberries, blackberries, redcurrants and strawberries, earlier in the summer, adding blackberries later on in the year. If you do not have fresh fruit available, use a bag of frozen summer fruits which you can find in the frozen food cabinets in large supermarkets. Serve with Fairy Cookies (p. 123) or Meringue Fingers (p. 124). Add the single cream if you want a richer, creamier result.

1. Put the fruits in a saucepan with the sugar and water and cook very gently until soft. Remove from the heat and crush the fruits a little with a potato masher. If you are using a lot of blackberries, you may like to sieve the fruit mixture to remove the seeds.

2. In a small bowl, mix the cornflour with a little water, or some juice from the pan, and add to the cooked fruits. Return to the heat and simmer gently to thicken the fondue. Add the cream if using, mixing well. Transfer to the fondue pot on the table and serve with the Fairy Cookies and Meringue Fingers for dipping.

YOU WILL NEED

450 g (1 lb) mixed summer fruits

100 g (4 oz) sugar

150 ml (5 fl oz) water

1 tbsp cornflour

150 ml (5 fl oz) single cream (optional)

TO SERVE

Fairy Cookies and Meringue Fingers

SERVES 4

STRAWBERRY FONDUE

Keep a tin of strawberries in natural juice in your store cupboard so you can make this fondue quickly and easily. Bright in colour, this is less rich than some and is served cold.

Drain the strawberries and put into the fondue pot with the grated orange rind. Mash with a fork, add the yoghurt and sugar to taste.

YOU WILL NEED

400 g (14 oz) tin of strawberries in natural juice

grated rind of an orange

400 g (14 oz) natural yoghurt (Greek yoghurt gives a creamier result)

sugar to taste

TO SERVE

Chocolate finger biscuits and Fairy Cookies (p. 123)

SERVES 4

COCONUT FONDUE

This unusual fondue is made with creamed coconut, which comes in a solid block. Serve with something crunchy like Mini Oatcakes (p. 126) for dipping.

1. Put the desiccated coconut into a saucepan with the water, creamed coconut and sugar over a medium heat. Bring to a simmer, and cook for ten minutes. Pour the mixture into a sieve over a bowl and press through well to strain the liquid.

2. Blend the cornflour with the milk in the fondue pot. Add the coconut liquid and warm through gently, stirring all the time.

YOU WILL NEED

75 g (3 oz) desiccated coconut

450 ml (15 fl oz) water

50 g (2 oz) creamed coconut, chopped

50 g (2 oz) sugar

1 tbsp cornflour

150 ml (5 fl oz) milk

TO SERVE
Mini Oatcakes

SERVES 4

TOFFEE FUDGE FONDUE

This rich, sticky sauce goes well with chocolate finger biscuits, boudoir cookies and fresh fruit. You can also serve it poured over ice cream.

YOU WILL NEED

100 g (4 oz) butter

100 g (4 oz) dark brown sugar

2 tbsp golden syrup

150 ml (5 fl oz) double cream

1 tsp vanilla extract

TO SERVE

Amaretti biscuits, fresh fruit and dried apricots

SERVES 4

1. Melt the butter in a pan over a low heat on the stove.

2. Add all the rest of the ingredients and bring to a low simmer. Cook for 4–5 minutes to thicken the fondue.

3. Transfer to the fondue pot on the table burner to keep warm. Serve with the biscuits and fruit for dipping.

FLUFFY MARSHMALLOW FONDUE

Fluffy marshmallows make a wonderful fondue melted with cream. Serve with something fruity and sharp, such as grapes or cherries for dipping.

Put the cream and marshmallows into the fondue pot over a gentle heat. Heat through, stirring constantly, until the marshmallows have melted. Add the sherry and serve warm with the fruit and Crunchy Chocolate Rice Cakes or chocolate finger biscuits.

YOU WILL NEED

150 g (6 oz) marshmallows

300 ml (10 fl oz) double cream

2 tbsp medium sherry

TO SERVE

Fruit or Crunchy Chocolate Rice Cakes (p. 127)

SERVES 4

SWEET DIPPERS

You can serve these sweet fondues with all sorts of accompaniments for dipping. Fresh fruits work well with most of the recipes – whole strawberries, cherries, pineapple chunks, slices of peaches and nectarines, chunks of melon – just use your imagination.

Try serving ready-made biscuits, like amaretti, chocolate finger biscuits, langue du chat and shortbread fingers. You could also serve chunks of trifle sponges, brandy snaps – again, use your imagination. Listed here are some recipes if you would prefer to make your own dippers.

Frozen Bananas ◀

Fairy Cookies ◀

Meringue Fingers ◀

Puff Pastry Twists ◀

Mini Oatcakes ◀

Crunchy Chocolate ◀
Rice Cakes

FROZEN
BANANAS

Frozen bananas taste like banana ice cream and are delicious with any chocolate-based fondue. Freeze the bananas the day before you need them – they do not keep for very long in the freezer.

Freeze one banana per person – put the whole banana in its skin in the freezer and leave overnight. Remove from the freezer ten minutes before needed. Peel the bananas, and cut into chunks.

FAIRY COOKIES

These little light sponge cookies are ideal for soaking up a fruity fondue.

YOU WILL NEED

3 eggs, separated
100 g (4 oz) sugar
1 tsp vanilla essence
100 g (4 oz) plain flour
pinch of salt

1. Pre-heat the oven to 160°C (325°F).

2. Put the egg yolks, sugar and vanilla essence into a large bowl. Beat together using an electric whisk, until the mixture becomes pale and thick and the beaters leave a ribbon trail when lifted.

3. Sift the flour and salt into a separate bowl. Whisk the egg whites until stiff in another bowl and fold into the egg mixture alternately with the flour.

4. Grease a baking tray and put spoonfuls of the mixture onto the tray. Bake in the oven for 8–10 minutes until light brown. Remove from the oven and leave on the tray for a minute or two. Cool on a wire rack.

MERINGUE FINGERS

These light fingers are ideal for dipping in any sweet fondue. Sprinkle with flaked almonds before cooking for added texture and flavour.

YOU WILL NEED

2 egg whites

pinch of cream of tartar

100 g (4 oz) sugar

25 g (1 oz) flaked almonds (optional)

MAKES 10-12 FINGERS

1. Preheat the oven to 130°C (275°F).

2. Put the egg whites and cream of tartar into a bowl and whisk with an electric whisk until stiff peaks are just forming and all the large bubbles have gone. Continue whisking, adding the sugar a little at a time, beating well between additions. Carry on whisking until all the sugar has been added and the mixture becomes glossy.

3. Lightly grease and flour a baking tray or line the tray with non-stick reusable liner. Using a piping bag with a wide nozzle, pipe fingers of meringue about 7.5 cm (3 in.) long, and sprinkle a few of the almonds on top of each finger.

4. Put the meringues into the oven and leave to cook for 1-2 hours. The longer you leave the meringues, the drier they become. Turn off the oven and leave the meringues in the oven until it has gone cold.

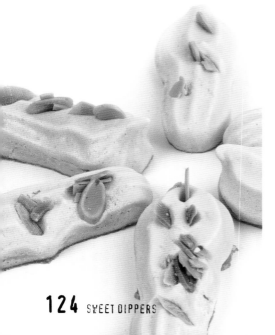

PUFF PASTRY
TWISTS

Use ready-made puff pastry to make
these pretty twists for dipping into any
sweet fondue. If you have a deep fat fryer
they are very quick to cook, or you can
cook them in the oven.

1. Roll out the pastry on a floured surface to a thickness of 1 cm
(½ in.). Use a sharp knife to cut strips about 10 cm (4 in.) long.

2. Put enough vegetable oil in a pan to deep fry the twists,
or use a deep fat fryer. Heat the oil to 190°C (375°F), or until
a piece of pastry dropped in the oil is sizzling and brown in
thirty seconds.

3. Twist the puff pastry strips and drop into the oil to cook. When
puffed up and golden, remove from the oil, drain, and place on a
paper towel. Dust liberally with sugar while still warm.

4. If you prefer, you can cook the pastry twists on a baking tray in
the oven at 200°C (400°F). Brush with the beaten egg and cook for
5–10 minutes until golden brown and puffed. Put on a wire rack
to cool and dust with sugar while still warm.

YOU WILL NEED

200 g (7 oz) ready-made puff pastry

plain flour for dusting

1 beaten egg

sugar for dusting

vegetable oil for frying

MINI
OATCAKES

Good for dunking in any of the sweet fondues.

YOU WILL NEED

150 g (6 oz) butter

2 tbsp golden syrup or clear honey

100 g (4 oz) demerara sugar

225 g (8 oz) oats

pinch salt

1 tsp vanilla extract

1. Preheat the oven to 180°C (350°F). Melt the butter, syrup, or honey, and sugar in a pan over a low heat until melted. Remove from the heat and add the oats, salt, and vanilla extract, mixing well.

2. Put the mixture into a greased 17.5 cm (7 in.) square tin. Bake in the oven until golden brown. Cut into small oblong pieces while still warm and leave to cool in the tin.

CRUNCHY CHOCOLATE
RICE CAKES

A great favourite with all ages, these are easy to make. Serve with Fluffy Marshmallow Fondue (p. 119).

YOU WILL NEED

50 g (2 oz) butter

2 tbsp golden syrup

50 g (2 oz) plain chocolate

75 g (3 oz) puffed rice breakfast cereal

1. Put the butter, golden syrup and chocolate into a pan over a low heat. Cook, stirring all the time until melted. Take off the heat and mix in the puffed rice.

2. Drop spoonfuls of the mixture into little petit fours or sweet paper cases and leave in the refrigerator until set.

HAVE FUN—HAVE A FONDUE!